SKETCHBOOKING

How to Create a Delightful Journal of Your Travels At Home or Abroad

BY BARBARA M. STECHER

This is the place where
Bob & I stayed for The 1989
Painting in France —

To my husband Bob

Edited by Gillian Nagler
Design by Glenn Suokko
Printed in Belgium

ISBN: 0945506341
Library of Congress: 2001090373

To order additional copies of this book,
please contact
The Store @ DeCordova
DeCordova Museum and Sculpture Park
51 Sandy Pond Road
Lincoln, MA 01773
Phone: (781) 259-8692
Fax: (781) 259-3650
Email: info@decordova.org
www.decordova.org

Acknowledgments

I hardly know where to begin because there has been so much encouragement and cheering from students, travelers, friends and family about my writing this book. I want to thank Anita McClellan, a literary agent who took my class and helped me edit an early version of the manuscript years ago. This initial effort was important background for proving my system in extensive travel situations.

Recently, I began a new manuscript. I want to thank my neighbor, Janet Tobin, for entering it into the computer, and her patience in doing it all over again when I decided on a total rewrite. Another neighbor, Mary Ann Hales, who has been watching my process over the years, helped us prepare the manuscript for presentation to a publisher (which is very generous considering that she is a publisher at Cottage Press!).

My wildest dream came true when Dr. Paul Master-Karnik, Director of DeCordova Museum and Sculpture Park, said that the Museum would like to publish the book!

Endless thanks are due to the staff members of New England's best contemporary art museum. Curatorial Fellow Gillian Nagler was assigned the task of editing, and helping me to prepare the materials to present to the designer Glenn Suokko. Much assistance was given by Corey Cronin, Marketing Director; Sarah Nosal, Marketing and Design Coordinator; and David Duddy, Director of Retail Operations for The Store @ DeCordova. Thanks also go to Linda Foster, Manager of the DeCordova Museum School of Art, who has scheduled and filled my classes over the years; and to Paul (again) for the Foreword to this book that integrates Sketchbooking into the overall educational mission of DeCordova.

Among the other people that I'd like to thank are Christine Ridout for writing magazine articles about Sketchbooking, and those who have invited me to do various Sketchbooking trips abroad: Dr. Seymour Simmons, Cynthia Hill, and Marion Carter. Thank you for so much fun!

BARBARA

Contents

II OFF TO

ALEXANDRIA →

passing by Giza with a glance!

This sketch of the pyramids at Giza was made as our bus was turning the corner. We didn't visit the pyramids until four days later, but I was eager to get them into my book.

Foreword

The DeCordova Museum School of Art was founded in 1950, at the same time as the Museum itself. The School, which was organized to provide a wide range of students with professional studio art education in a non-degree-granting context, was an integral part of the DeCordova mission. DeCordova's program was definitely populist, dedicated to bringing "living" contemporary art to as broad a public as possible. Our philosophy has been that the creative process of the artist is genuinely open to all comers. It just takes time and commitment, along with skill and intellect, to gain entry into the world of art making which can also open the door to greater art appreciation.

This beautiful small volume, *Sketchbooking* by Barbara Stecher, wonderfully demonstrates this broad-based philosophy of education at work. Stecher's approach to drawing addresses the potential artist in us all, and encourages us to begin accessing that potential. To summarize her message to any individual who might casually pick up this book and consider its contents, "just do it" seems the appropriate phrase.

Most importantly, *Sketchbooking* is more than simply another "how to" series of instructions. The essence of *Sketchbooking* is genuinely a frame of mind, or perhaps a conditioning of mind, that encourages us to be "in the moment" as much as possible—to borrow the acting metaphor. This book challenges the reader to become an activist by embracing the immediate environment (whatever it might happen to be) in direct and visually expressed terms. Sketchbooking is truly an adventure in visual education, and the enhanced understanding of our world that can be gained through interpreting its representation. And isn't that what art making is really all about.

Paul Master-Karnik
Director
DeCordova Museum and Sculpture Park

Introduction

I am a traveler. After a trip, I want someone to know how much fun I had, and what nifty things I did and saw. Most of all, though, I want to be reminded of the in-between moments, and the details that are so easily forgotten.

I began making sketchbooks because I could not find time to paint while traveling. I used to take my painting paraphernalia along when my husband Bob and I began to travel, but it added weight to our luggage, an element of frustration to our sightseeing, and I would return home and sigh, "Why didn't I paint?"

On the next trip I left my paints at home, but kept a written journal. Bob watched me dutifully making entries and said, "Why not sketch?" It was six in the evening, we were in the car about to drive away, and to show how impractical sketching was, I started to draw the scene in my journal. To my surprise, in ten minutes I had a wonderful little picture of Neuschwanstein. That sketch has brought back the whole experience of being there more than the words in the journal ever could.

The next trip took us to China. I was *sure* I could paint something there. I took a small painting kit and carried it to the highest

Just to prove it couldn't be done, I sketched this view of the Neuschwanstein Castle from the car. I was surprised by the results!

3

This sketch captured the excitement of being at the highest point on the Great Wall of China.

Barb making a watercolor from the high point of the Great China Wall
Oct 1, 1984

Lever Barb Bob

point on the Great Wall. For the few minutes available before reboarding the bus, I painted! It was a thrill to be there, fulfilling my dream. I was so excited about it that I drew the event in a 6 x 4-inch sketchbook I had begun to keep. I found that it was the experience I treasured more than the not-so-great painting I had made. That was the day the idea of *SKETCHBOOKING*—a word I made up—crystallized for me.

SKETCHBOOKING is an attitude, an approach to sketching that means that you carry a book and watch for moments to use it. There are often times to sketch if you have your kit at hand. Sketchbooking also means that you set up the book to be like a published book, with a title page, chapters, etc. The book is totally self-explanatory, now or years from now.

The difference between this concept and an artist's or traveler's sketchbook is this: the book is not a collection of fine drawings. Rather, it is a record of my journey that may include some fine drawings. It includes what I did, my adventure, and the great monuments I saw. It is an opportunity for both sketching and journalizing. I feel at ease because nobody will see the book unless I allow it.

Since 1988, I have taught a short course called SKETCHBOOK-ING. It is time to put the concept into a book for you. I will use my own sketches to illustrate what I mean. I have been lucky enough to travel to all seven continents, and I have a shelf full of sketchbooks about the journeys.

I hope that you will enjoy Sketchbooking too.

Include things that amuse you. In Kaunakakai, Molokai, I heard giggling coming from a tree. It turned out that it was full of laughing children.

CHAPTER I

How Sketchbooking Works

Traditionally one fills a sketchbook with drawings to carefully recreate a scene. For example, if you were doing a book about Washington, DC, your book would have good sketches of the famous sites. Page after page would have familiar and expected subjects. That is possible if you have the time and the skill.

Sketchbooking is different. It takes less time, less skill, and is about much more than the famous sights. It is about your experience, your observations, your being there. For example, on your visit to the Lincoln Memorial, you might have eaten a bag lunch while sitting on the steps. Draw yourself doing that, with the columns as background and Mr. Lincoln looking over your shoulder from the distance.

Then go inside and make a few sketches there. Perhaps sketch some kids looking up, up, up to see the kindly face. Add a quote from the wall. Show the view looking out and write, "This is what Mr. Lincoln looks at all day." Your sketch might show the nation's Capitol in the distance. Write the thoughts that pop into your head. These spontaneous reactions are better than a statement that you struggle to put into words about how important the man was. And, probably as you approach or leave the area, you will sketch the whole monument from the distance—not a formal drawing, just a loving sketch. Or, your sketch, if you are there on a tour, will be different.

It might be one sketch to remember being there.

In either scenario, you cannot necessarily plan ahead. Use the time at hand. If you want to make a long sketch, do it. Your book will be fun to read because it will have various kinds of sketches and an unconventional plot.

While other people are busy snapping photos, you are creating a Sketchbook.

BUT CAN I DRAW WELL ENOUGH?

People can derive a lot of pleasure from drawing. When someone says to me, "I wish I could draw," my response is, "If you want to, go ahead and draw!" That is what this book is all about. Many people will not try to draw because they are unwilling to risk being embarrassed, or they simply feel a little silly about wanting to. They will not pick up a drawing pencil because they do not consider themselves to be artists. Few of my students aspire to being artists, but they would like to be able to draw with confidence.

In Sketchbooking you will learn that there is a wonderful experience available to you regardless of what your drawings look like. Many of the benefits of being an artist are possible to enjoy without being a professional.

Sketchbooking can give you:
- a new way of "seeing" the world around you.
- the fun of making something of what you see.

To realize these possibilities, it is important to ACCEPT THE

WAY YOU DRAW AT ANY GIVEN MOMENT—now or ten years from now. Let this be your drawing style. If a drawing looks like that of a five-year-old, that's OK. A five-year-old artist has a freedom of expression that gets ideas across, and enjoys the process. Your skill will improve. Regardless of what you think of your present ability to draw, the important thing is to begin.

A bonus you may not expect is that this sketching effort also leads you to a deeper appreciation of art. One student excitedly explained, "I went to an exhibition of master drawings. I have never enjoyed an exhibition so much before, all because I, too, had been drawing! I saw them with new comprehension."

Drawing is an art. Sketchbooking is an art, too. It is more casual. It is storytelling.

LET'S SKETCH!

Begin sketching now, today. Do not wait to make time for it. Your life is probably already over-scheduled. Keep a sketchbook in your pocket. Sketch in "found" times: on the train, waiting for lunch to arrive, or on your break. Thus, formerly lost moments become opportunities to sketch.

If you mess up, who cares? Don't worry. Even art students think that absolutely everyone else draws better than they do. Have a laugh, write a few words and keep on sketching. Your "mess-ups" could become the best part of the sketchbook. Mess up, but do not give up! As you proceed, your sketching will improve. You are at the beginning of an adventure.

Make sketching an active part of your life. Rather than deciding to devote a set time each day to drawing, live by spontaneity and inspiration. See each day as a glorious opportunity for creativity. There is no need to turn out 365 sketches a year, or even 100. Always have your sketchbook handy and stay aware of the world around you.

SKETCHES ARE LIKE WILDFLOWERS

They must be free, unconstrained.
They grow anywhere.
They are beautiful.
They have great variety.
They are found in unexpected places.
They are to be enjoyed, looked at.
They are very special.

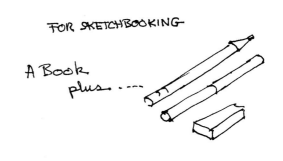

FOR SKETCHBOOKING

A Book
plus ----

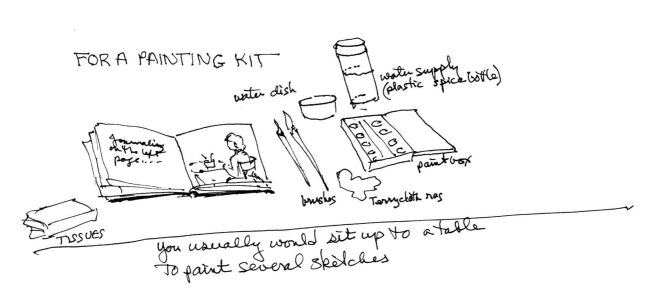

FOR A PAINTING KIT

water dish

water supply
(plastic spice bottle)

Journaling
on the left
page ...

paint box

brushes   Terrycloth rag

TISSUES

You usually would sit up to a table
To paint several sketches

*This sketch shows how I lay out
supplies when I set up to paint a
few sketches.*

CHAPTER TWO

Getting Started

SUPPLIES YOU WILL NEED

Art stores have the items you will need: a book, a pen, a pencil, an eraser, and a little paint box. The idea is to travel light, to have exactly what you need, and no more.

Pencil
 A 2B or 3B drawing pencil

Eraser
 Buy a white plastic eraser like a Staedtler–Mars Plastic. An art gum works well but leaves crumbs. The eraser on the end of a pencil is too harsh and will damage the paper.

Pen with black ink
 There are all kinds of good pens out there—just be sure that the ink line cannot be seen even faintly through the back of the page. A reliable pen is the Pilot Precise Rolling Ball extra fine, black ink. The ink flows smoothly, the pen always works, and you can buy

them almost anywhere. The ink is not waterproof, however, and will sometimes run as you paint a sketch.

For a waterproof pen, use one labeled Pigma Micron—the ink is both waterproof and fade proof. These pens come in various line widths. I find that 03 is a good size.

Sketchbook

One of the pleasures of Sketchbooking is selecting blank books. Many types of books are offered now—paperback or softbound; hardback black books in many shapes and sizes; and beautiful hand-made books with attractive covers and exotic papers. As I browse the art supply stores, I buy any books that appeal to me, and I have on hand various sizes and types. I enjoy having them, and the right one is usually there when I decide to start a new sketchbook.

Spiral-bound sketchbooks are less appropriate for Sketchbook-ing because it is too easy to rip pages out. As your bound book fills, you will be encouraged to keep it going.

Buy only quality books. The paper should be pH neutral (acid free or archival quality), or it will eventually yellow. Do not buy a "practice book." You do not need practice in sketching—you are doing it now! From the moment you start, your work counts. Fur-thermore, your sketching will look better because it is on good paper.

The paper must be heavy enough so ink lines will not show through to the back of a page. A smooth finish is more pleasant to draw on than one that is rough or feels slightly pulpy. Cachet Prod-ucts, Inc. has an assortment of bound books. A good one to use for Sketchbooking is 9 x 6 inches, has 212 pages, and a paper weight of

65 lb. When you have 212 pages, you won't have to worry about running out of paper. The pages are wider than they are tall (landscape format), and feel natural for drawing.

Your choice of book size will depend on the use you will make of it. If you are going mountain climbing or getting in and out of small boats, get one that fits in your pocket. If you are on a month-long trip, consider an 8 x 7-inch Pentalic Sketch Journal made by M. Grumbacher, Inc. which has a sturdy cover and 192 pages. Select a book that you are willing to carry, a size that can be in your bag or pocket for day-to-day sketching opportunities.

A book larger than 10 x 8 inches is huge when open and tends to announce loudly that you are sketching. Large pages get beyond sketch journals and become places for ambitious drawings that are harder to do well.

Sometimes I'll buy a book in a very non-standard shape. For example, I recorded the story of a week's vacation in an accordion-pleated Japanese book with tall, narrow pages. It is a lively book and you never know quite where to begin looking at it. Definitely a change of pace! It can even stand open on a shelf to show several sketches at a time.

A small painting kit

Put together a painting kit that has everything you need, ready to use:

- A sketcher's watercolor set
- A good quality #10 watercolor brush
- A bottle for water—a 2-ounce plastic spice bottle works (don't forget to test it for leaking!)

- Water dish—a low, plastic one for dipping your brush
- A small rag—cut up a white washcloth
- A package of tissues

Finally, get something to carry your paint supplies in, perhaps a clear plastic makeup kit from the drugstore. The kit should fit into your sketching bag, although you will usually leave the paints at the hotel to lighten your load.

Brushes

The array of brushes displayed at the art store is overwhelming. Ask for help from a knowledgeable person. Watercolor brushes that look alike can have wildly different price tags, depending how and of what materials they were made. The brush you buy must come to a point when it is wet (the store will let you test it by dipping it into water), and must spring back into shape when bent. These characteristics give you control as you paint.

People think they need brushes in a range of sizes and will buy a set. Not only is it a nuisance to be shifting from one brush to another, it is unnecessary. Get one good brush (I recommend a size #10) that will hold enough paint for large areas, but also comes to a fine point for details. Get the best brush you can afford.

Paint Boxes

You can get a sketcher's paint box ready to use, about 3 x 5 inches in size. Winsor & Newton has a line of small watercolor sets ranging from a plastic box with cakes of student-grade colors and a paintbrush, to one with the finest quality artist's color, a metal box, and brush for about ten times the cost. An artist who already has tubes of watercolor paints can make a paint box by filling a small plastic folding palette.

See what your art supply store has. Paints are an investment. Your time and efforts are worth good-quality materials.

The Sketcher's Travel Kit

Assemble a kit for your trip. It will be exactly the same as the one you use at home, except that you will take extra pens and pencils, and you will need to add a very small pencil sharpener. Because pens will occasionally leak on a flight, be sure to wrap them in a plastic bag. And remember to bring along your paints!

Use a shoulder bag or a fanny pack that fits the book you plan to take, and use it as a purse for whatever else you need to carry. Travel as light as possible, because a heavy bag will wear you down. A SportSac shoulder bag works because it is reliably sturdy, lightweight, and comes in various sizes and colors. Your hands are free and everything you need is at your disposal. When you want to sketch, you are ready in 30 seconds. Devise a system that meets your needs.

SETTING UP FOR CREATIVITY

This section demonstrates how to set up a sketchbook. Setting up your sketchbook much like you would a regular book is essential to the concept of Sketchbooking. Proceed with confidence—make

SETTING UP FOR CREATIVITY

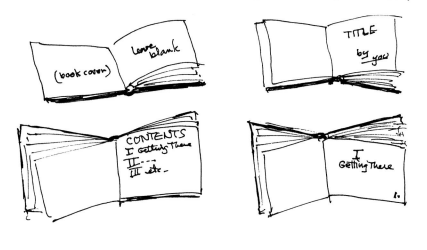

Follow this basic format for setting up your sketchbook.

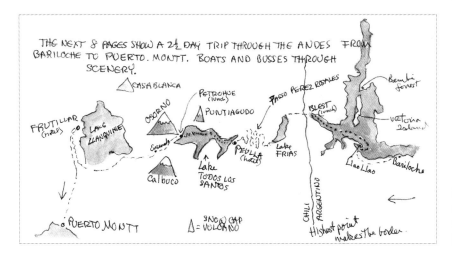

Include maps wherever you feel they are needed. I often put one just after the contents page to show the whole itinerary.

it just like a published book.

Leave the first page blank. Pretty easy so far!

The second right-hand page is the TITLE PAGE. Give your book a title, and personalize it by adding, "A Sketchbook by … you."

Put your INTRODUCTION on the third right-hand page. Write a chatty paragraph about your reason for making this particular sketchbook.

At the top of the next right-hand page print CONTENTS. Add chapter titles here as your book develops.

Save the following page for a hand drawn map of your itinerary.

On the next right-hand page, write CHAPTER ONE and the title of your first chapter.

The next right-hand page is where you begin sketching. Sketches should generally be made on the right-hand page of your book in order to avoid drawing on the back of another sketch, to prevent overcrowding, and to leave space for journal entries. There are exceptions, of course, but it is helpful to begin this way.

Each chapter might refer to a new destination, a new day, or a new event. Chapters encourage you to wrap up a sequence of sketches, to finish your work on an idea or an event or a place. Add every chapter title to the Contents page as the book grows. The pages can be numbered later.

So, that is the setting-up process that gives your book a structured format. Using the pattern of a published book will offer you a context for your creativity.

When you can, sit down and sketch to your heart's content. Though I could have spent hours on this view of Mesa Verde, completing the sketch took me about fifteen minutes.

Sample Cliff Palace

MESA VERDE

CHAPTER THREE

The Basics of Sketching

Wherever you go, take your sketchbook along. Let yourself be free; just walk or sit—listen to, look at, and feel where you are.

Do not look around frantically for a subject to sketch. Leave your "organized" self at home. Simply be where you are. Enjoy— let go. You might feel more like a poet than a sketcher. Write a line, make some observations, and soon, something will attract your attention and you will begin sketching. Your experience of the place is enriched because the sketching enhances your perceptions. The results will have more heart than if you had plunked yourself down saying, "Gotta get this scene into my book."

Your creativity surfaces when you let go of your preconceptions. The idea is not necessarily to be organized, but to be organized just enough to give your creativity a chance.

HERE'S HOW

You rarely sketch at a table. Usually you will have the sketchbook in your lap, or you'll be holding the book as you stand, perhaps leaning it on something convenient. Lightly begin a very simple drawing.

Hold the pencil *loosely* in your hand. Start sketching as you observe the subject. When your confidence grows, reinforce the lines, become more definite. Do not erase as you go along—it can interrupt your concentration. It does not matter how many wrong lines you make. Just draw over your "mistakes." Your pencil lines must be light enough to erase later.

The minute you feel that the drawing is developing, put the pencil down and continue to sketch in ink. Yes, *ink*! Ink over the pencil lines that you like or freely draw new lines, and add the details. Then gently erase the pencil lines. If you need to add anything, draw more.

Perhaps you are looking at a scene. You have the urge to sketch it. You are overwhelmed by its complexity; it is too much! Focus your attention on one object. Draw that.

You can stop there, or you can expand the drawing by attaching the surroundings, using the one object as a measure for all the rest. If I just draw a big rock, what is the point? But as I draw this one at the edge of my patio, I smile. As I sketch it, I recall how we have nursed that little azalea along (the one on the left; the other one has always been there). I must include the area in front of the rock; it is my bulb garden. If I want the whole scene, I let the sketch grow. I relate everything else to the rock. Compositionally speaking, the rock is the center of interest. I do not, however, simply plop the "center of interest" in the center of the page. With just a little advance thinking and a little trial-and-error with the pencil, I find a satisfying composition.

This gentle approach will take you far. Start with the part you

Start your sketch by drawing the object that interests you. Attach more of its surroundings if you like.

know, and the rest will come. Let your sketch grow.

When you sketch, have the pencil in your writing hand, and the pen and eraser in the other hand that is also supporting the book. This way, you have everything you need available to you. When it is time to switch from the pencil to the pen, you do not have to interrupt your concentration to stop and find it.

At first you may find that switching from pencil to pen is difficult, even scary. In my class, a leader in industry exclaimed, "Switch to ink? You can't be serious!" You will be surprised at how much better a sketch becomes as you change those tentative pencil lines into ink. If you become unsure while using the pen, switch back to the pencil to solve the drawing problem. Then return to the pen again to finish the sketch in ink. Take a few seconds to gently erase the pencil lines.

Keep in mind that you do not need to draw everything in sight. You may be tempted to draw a hundred leaves in pencil. What a chore then, to have to ink each one! You rarely have to draw all those leaves anyway, or all the shingles on the roof, or all the bricks on the house. If you draw just a few, it will be enough to indicate that the house is brick, the roof is shingled, etc. Aim for simplicity. You want just enough to convey the idea, not to tell everything there is to know. Go for a simple line sketch rather than a complex drawing.

Again, hold your pencil loosely. Make as many lines as you need. Many will not be right, but you will find the lines that work. Make the switch early from pencil to pen. Do not be a slave to the pencil line. Use it or draw a better, more definitive one in ink. Otherwise you are doing the sketch twice, once in pencil, and once in pen.

North end of Zocalo
The Magnificent METROPOLITAN CATHEDRAL begun by Cortez — Foundations of present

This cathedral in Mexico City was so complex that I didn't know where to focus. You can see the tentative pencil lines as I tried to find my way. When your eye doesn't know where to begin, just enjoy looking and soon it will come to you!

Resist the temptation to use shading and crosshatching. Simple lines make good sketches and lend themselves to color if you decide to paint them later.

Write something near each sketch or on the facing page. Words written at the time are always better than those you agonize over later. Decide where the writing belongs as part of the overall composition. The location varies from sketch to sketch. Sometimes the words go right on the sketch page; other times, you will decide to do most of your writing on the adjacent page. There is no rule. Some journal keepers write everywhere and scatter sketches through the text. Suit yourself. Just be sure that you write *something, somewhere, as you go along.*

There are variations in page layout that will give flexibility in your sketching and add a more dynamic element to your book. Though these may require that you draw on the back of another sketch, you will be doing it for a reason—not just as a means to save paper.

- **Double Page:** Some scenes, such as a sunrise over the Himalayas or the Fourth of July parade on Main Street, will require a full double-page spread.
- **Spill-over Page**: Occasionally a sketch will outgrow its space and spill over partly onto the other page.
- **Vignette Page**: Sometimes you will put several little sketches on the same page, as when some subjects belong together, they flash by quickly, or they simply do not need a whole page.

pages: 26–27: This view of Mt. Etna is an example of a scene that was best represented in a double-page layout.

Greek Theatre at Taormina   It's not quit this close!

BALI

TV DISHES
aim straight up.

School children.
Once a week they take
buckets to clean the school

field worker

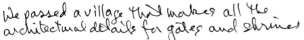
DUCKS

We passed a village that makes all the
architectural details for gates and shrines .

Driving is an experience. Our driver
was excellent, never took a chance. However
he passed every car on the road. Drove
close (inches) from motor scooters, but
the bikers seem to expect it. Every
vehicle on the road is in close quarters.
Since we couldn't do a thing about it,
we relaxed, rather than being terrified!

This illustrates a typical vignette page.

- **Vertical Page**: On some occasions your sketch will require that you turn the book on end to compose a tall, tall subject.

Remember also to vary the scale of your sketches. Five consecutive panoramas of the Grand Canyon, with nary a flower or a person in close-up, could be tedious.

DRAWING PEOPLE

If the idea of drawing people and of getting a likeness intimidates you, you are not alone. But being terrified is no excuse! What if the prehistoric cave artists had waited until they could do people better? What about Picasso? Even Michelangelo was not concerned about getting a likeness. When he carved the figure of Duke Giuliano for the Medici tomb, his patron complained that the portrait did not look like the Duke. Michelangelo replied that in 1000 years, no one would care.

A sketchbook inevitably includes drawings of people you do not know. This is an opportunity to gain experience with drawing figures and faces. If the faces do not look like the people, it doesn't matter. The important thing is to capture the attitude, gesture, or mood. When you are including friends, and you really want the likeness, take it easy. You can ruin a drawing by over-working the face in an attempt to get it right. Select a position of the person that clearly catches his attitude, one that highlights his big jacket or floppy hat. The face should be a small part simply drawn. Take every

Liz relaxes enroute --
is reading
Maiden Voyage by Tania Aebi

At one point I wept over the beauty of the land and sky & clouds. I must keep on traveling because I so love & enjoy what I see & do..... the sights + sites. Traveling as an artist is my way. It sharpens the experience + is fun.

When you draw people, you don't have to worry about capturing an exact likeness. These two sketches show the same person, Liz, using different amounts of detail.

Liz leaps
for joy --

opportunity to draw faces and heads. Have the courage to include people at every turn in your story. Make sure that you draw yourself in some of the scenes.

The technique is the same for drawing animals. In preparation for a trip to East Africa, I bought a book on how to draw animals. The book was fascinating, but I could not master it in time for the trip. I decided I would have to be satisfied with my own on-the-spot renditions. On safari, I had the time of my life drawing animals in the same way I approach all other sketching. And you can tell perfectly well that my elephant is an elephant.

No person or animal will stand still for you. Never mind; catch what you can and let nothing discourage you from completing your sketch in some form. If you have to change the sketch a bit, you can!

Rhinoceri in the Ngorogoro Crater in Tanzania. I penciled them in lightly, then switched to pen to improve the drawing as I continued observing the animals.

SKETCHING ON THE RUN

In the spirit of Sketchbooking, you will be sketching at odd times and in inconvenient places. Often your work will have to be done quickly, but you should not feel rushed. If you have only three minutes, relax and use the whole three minutes. Do your best to get some ink on it. Use the time as if you had all day. You will find that you can catch the essence of a scene quickly. When there is something you want in your book and there is virtually no time to capture it, start sketching anyway. So often, the time available ends up being longer than you'd expected.

When you are passing something along the road, freeze a mental snapshot and immediately sketch it as well as you can, perhaps with

a mere scribble. Add a few words, and later you will be surprised at how much those few lines bring back to you.

You may also find yourself in a situation where you are standing still but your subject is not. "He moved," you say in despair. That's OK, because he will probably move through the same position again and again. Begin the sketch by catching the gesture you want to show. Then watch for the subject to move through the pose again, and get the details you need—the arm, the bend of the leg—and bit by bit you will have it. When you ink it, you will easily select the best lines or maybe add new ones; the eraser will dispose of the rest.

A good way to sketch an active subject such as a workman, a tennis player, or a child at play is to draw three or four poses at the same time, on the same page or on a double page, catching whatever fits. This is fun to do. Try it. See what you get.

There will be times when you have to shift into high gear to catch all the information you want for your book, and you'll have to scramble, sketching as you can. Under this pressure, you will not have time to finish as you go through the day. You should still keep both pencil and pen in your hand, and switch to ink whenever possible. Do what you have to do in order to get the sense of each subject. Let mistakes sit there and keep on sketching to capture the spirit of the moment. You will discover that you'll do well in this absorbing situation because you will not have time for any self-sabotaging criticism: "Am I doing this right?" or "This sketch is not good." You will rise to the occasion—sketch excitedly, even wildly, but never feel rushed. Get some ink on it! You will have a great time.

View of a busy street in Paris. I just kept adding things that caught my attention.

In a demanding situation, your sketches may look pretty bad to you. Keep sketching regardless, because you are capturing the feel of the moment. The alternative is to have nothing. Your sketches reflect the occasion, leisurely or frantic. Finish them as soon as possible while the images are still fresh in your mind. Do it while you are still excited and "there." Add whatever is needed—ink, erase, comments, story line—until you are satisfied. This rapid sequence of sketches will look different from those made when you had tons of time, and the change of pace enriches the book.

You will discover that you can make competent sketches in a relatively short time, without fanfare or great preparation. On the spot, anywhere, be ready to sketch. That is Sketchbooking!

ADDING COLOR

Color can be a delightful addition to a sketchbook. If you have not painted since the third grade, do not worry. Just start on your least favorite sketch in your book, and see how much a little color can improve it. This is not proper watercolor painting. You are simply tinting the drawings gently, and as little as possible. Your painting experience is an advantage, but those without that experience will be successful too.

When to Paint

If you have an occasion to paint on location, do it. But usually, while traveling, you will concentrate on drawing. You could make a few color notes where you feel the exact color matters.

This drawing of Luxor Temple in Egypt shows how a little color can enliven an otherwise "not so great" sketch.

Sailing by Luxor Temple

Then, every few days, add the color to several sketches at a sitting. Sit at a table. Put the sketchbook right in front of you. Have your paint box, brushes, water container, and a rag laid out.

Which to Paint

There is no rule; just paint the sketches you want to paint. The book should be a random combination of black-and-white and painted pages. Do not paint a wonderful sketch. You have achieved your goal in black and white, so leave it alone.

I begin each painting session by choosing a not-so-great sketch somewhere well into the book. This allows me to warm up to the painting process in a place that is safe—not a favorite sketch, and not the first one in the book. Also, my confidence grows because I have improved a poor and needy sketch. Then I go wherever I want in the book and paint to my heart's content. Actually, I have to restrain myself from painting everything in sight.

I like to brighten the title page and to put a stroke of color on the other setup pages. For example, I drag a color, one swipe of the loaded brush, over the word "Contents."

How to Paint

Wake up your paints by touching each color pan with a wet brush.

Your aim is to brighten your sketches by adding a little color. Take it easy. See how little paint you can use to get the effect you want. You can always add more. The color may be subdued or bright, as you wish, but should never be thick or heavy.

Use just a tad of water. The paper in the sketchbook is relatively thin and smooth, and it will not take a wet slosh of water.

Begin painting in a safe area of the page and see your confidence develop. For example, with a figure, paint the legs before you do the face to see how the color looks. Be careful—the ink may run when wet by the paint. Have a tissue handy to blot it quickly. Begin to paint somewhere that a little "run" will not matter. Often you get an unexpectedly wonderful effect.

Check the other side of the page to be sure the color is not soaking through. If it is, you are using too much water. Also, if your page is undulating more than just a little, you'll know you are overdoing the water. All that extra water is not putting color on the page. The amount of pigment you pick up on the brush and deposit on the paper is what determines the color. The water just helps you spread it around.

When you load the brush with color, test it on the palette side of your paint box which is white like the paper. Change the color slightly from the pure colors in the set. A bit of blue or yellow in the green, for example, gives you a variety of greens to work with. If you always use color straight from the pan, your paintings will all look alike, with the same green everywhere. Greens are the hardest to make look natural. Avoid pool table green or swimming pool green unless you are in the Caribbean. Change red with a touch of yellow or blue. Use the white of the paper for white. Experiment.

Painting is a relatively quick operation. Use your #10 brush; a tiny brush forces you to take forever on a sketch. The larger brush makes painting a straightforward pleasure, and if of good quality, will also come to a fine point to handle the details. When you think a page is dry, lay a tissue on it before turning the page. Paint several pages at a sitting. If you spend a half hour per sketch, you will never finish!

When you are finished, close the book, with several tissues hanging out, and put something heavy on it for a few hours. This flattens the pages that may have become wavy from the water.

SKETCH SAVING

A fast, page-turning sketching session may produce some sketches that are not as good as you would like them to be. You know you could have done better with only a little more time. You are tempted to rip the whole batch right out of the book. HOLD ON! You are on to a special phase of Sketchbooking! Think of how dull your book would be if you left out occasions that did not provide time for a "proper" sketch.

Quickly-caught sketches exhibit a looser style; you may not even recognize them as your own. Several sketches in a sequence page after page support each other. They work together to make up the story. Later, when you come back to them, you will say, "Hey, these are pretty good!" A little passing of time helps you to be less critical of your work. Finish up a sequence in the spirit of the occasion.

In short, I recommend that pages not be removed from your book until it is almost finished. Early on, you cannot be a good judge of your own work. In the excitement of doing a sketch or a series of sketches, you do not always realize how well you are doing, or that your style is high art. At first, you may not even know what is good. Do not ask anyone else to decide for you. By the time the book is filled, you will have a lot of experience. *You* will have learned a lot. You will recognize a sketch that bothers you. Some sketches are bad! Despair not!

Before cutting the bad sketch out of the book, try *sketch saving*. You have everything to gain by working to improve your sketch. You have a very real possibility of turning the bad one into an acceptable one. I find that a *little* color helps clarify even the most vague sketch. Draw on it, too; work with it. If you totally fail, you can always remove the page, but keeping it may be important to your story, so try. You can learn a lot in these sketch saving ventures.

Remove a page if it really bothers you, or if you crinkle up inside when someone sees it. Then you will make no apologies for the book.

REMOVING A SKETCH

The way to remove a page, if necessary, is to use a sharp-edged cutter or a single-edged razor blade. Put a piece of cardboard under the page to cut against to protect the next page. Cut carefully, leaving about 1/3 inch of the page next to the binding. Otherwise, the page at the other part of the book will also come out.

DO NOT GIVE UP

On a fine, two-week tour of Egypt, I sketched happily, intending to make the best book yet. After all, I knew how to do it!!! This would be the textbook example. I was doing pretty well, I thought, but when I looked at the book at home, it was, well, hopelessly incomplete. There were many good sketches, some in color, but others were half done, only hinting at the experience that had been so fresh and exciting at the time.

The instruction I give to my classes, "when you get home, take time to re-read your book, make a few additions," usually works, but this time the task seemed overwhelming. I put the book aside, probably never to be seen again.

Then a phone call came from across the continent. "Grandmother, I told the teacher you made a sketchbook in Egypt. She wants you to show it to my sixth grade class."

"Sure, Honey." That was motivation I needed. I retrieved the book and got to work. I had scores of sketches, but many could benefit from sketch saving tactics. I worked for a week on the book, finishing the sketches, researching facts, getting the spelling right, completing details by referring to tour folder photos, and writing more entries. At last, I was happy with the book. Once I got started, I enjoyed doing it.

The message of this story is, **don't give up**. As I look at it today, I wonder how I could possibly have abandoned the book.

CHAPTER FOUR

Sketchbooking on Your Trip

Before you go on a trip, think about the sketch journal you want to make, get the appropriate supplies, and devise a practical way to carry them. After the sketching kit is settled, you can deal with the lesser details—passport, wardrobe, etc.

STARTING YOUR BOOK

People return from a trip excited about their filled sketchbooks—or with an empty book and the excuses for not doing it. Successful books are usually those that were started just before the trip. Let the title page reflect your excitement about your travel plans. The introduction page can tell why you are taking this trip, and that you are going to make your first travel sketchbook. Smile as you print CONTENTS on the next page, anticipating the great chapters to be entered there. Save the next right-hand page for a hand-drawn map of your itinerary. The following page announces "Chapter One—Getting There."

Turn to the next page (this will be the 7th right-hand page) and begin sketching. Show that you are getting ready for the trip. Draw yourself packing, all that stuff on the bed. Are you taking a bicycle? If it is a camping trip, show the car being loaded. Make another sketch of driving off.

The important thing to do is to get the book started!!!

If you are traveling by plane, include the airport in your story. Draw your companion checking in and yourself waiting. Include the general public in the scenes. Have some fun drawing people.

When you are on the plane, your sketch kit should be at hand for making a couple of in-flight sketches. This gets you into the swing of sketching. Include going through customs. What a scene! You will have to be fast; people keep moving. Catch their body language as they try to get out of the airport. Include those beyond the immigration point holding the greeting signs, especially if one has your name on it. Show yourself surrounded by luggage, waiting for transportation.

While most individual sketches are not very important in and of themselves, all your sketches together tell the story of the trip from the beginning. By including the little funny or rough things that happen, your start is light-hearted enough so that now anything you put in the book is fine.

Though I hesitate to admit this, I do not always succeed in getting my book started at home and have to do it on the plane. Once on board, I scan the in-flight magazine, close my eyes, relax. Then I begin to think about the sketchbook I want to make. My kit is at hand—I just reach into my bag for it. At my leisure, I set up the book, write, make sketches about the getaway from memory, and begin the live sketching where I am.

Call your first chapter GETTING THERE. It helps to get your book started before you actually leave for your trip. Draw yourself packing and getting ready to go.

CHAPTER I

Getting There

The woolly Mamouth watches...
Packing! Again--
Does it ever get easier?

Breakfast —
  Apricots, peaches, plums
  Brioche
  Cereal
  Sometimes croissants
  Coffee
  Yogurt
  Home made jam

*opposite: You'll usually have some
free time while waiting in airports.
Use this as a chance to sketch!*

*Let your first sketch be an easy one,
like food on the breakfast table.
Remember that everything is
important and worth sketching.*

There is a natural impulse to wait to begin a sketch journal at your destination, and you may choose to do so. If so, I advise that you begin absolutely on the first day, no later than breakfast. Draw something that feels easy to you. If you wait too long, you will be looking for something "worthy" of being first in the book, and believe it or not, a day or two may go by, and you might give up the book altogether.

I repeat: let your first sketch be an easy one—the geraniums, the coffeepot, the croissants. Your book will be started, and you will not be faced with the Eiffel Tower as your first sketch. From here on your interest, devotion, and enjoyment will carry you along as you sketch and journalize to your heart's content.

SEEING THE SIGHTS

When you are eager to see everything, you may not want to stop to sketch. I have solved this problem by stopping to make one sketch to show, for example, that we are in the Louvre. Then I put the book away and enjoy being there. Soon something strikes me that must get into the book. Although I have done my one "required" sketch, several more will spontaneously appear in the book. The additions begin to make the visit to the museum into the story of being there. Travelers in general should sit occasionally to see things, rather than sightseeing at a dead run. These leisurely interludes are good sketching times. But, you will also do sketches under more difficult circumstances. The fun of capturing something overcomes some inconvenience.

*Wat Phra temple in Thailand.
I relaxed and sketched without worry
or rush, which helped me to observe
this complex site.*

WAT Phra That Doi Suthep - a stunning sight

If you cannot finish a sketch on location, complete it when you can, preferably before you sleep. Finish while the experience is fresh in your mind. You will soon reach your own stride, and sketching along the way will be quite natural.

Sketch what you want, not what you think you ought to. Capture the adventurous aspects of your travel. Did you walk across the pond in Japan on stepping-stones? Show yourself doing it, almost falling in. Show the Southern Cross in the sky over Bolivia and Orion standing upside down on his hands—and put yourself in as a stargazer. Did you wade in the Indian Ocean? Sketch it! There are no demands here, except that you enjoy what you are doing.

Because most things travelers are seeing have been photographed a million times, you need not worry about getting it all perfectly. Do not copy Big Ben from a postcard. Your original sketch is far better, and sketching helps you see it better. The sketch is evidence of your being there.

Sketching and writing as you go enlivens your experience. This makes you into a more observant sightseer. Capture reactions while they are still fresh in your mind.

You might worry about keeping your travel companions waiting. In reality, they will probably be off buying the picnic lunch, studying the guidebook, doing a crossword, or taking photographs. Your sketching will hit a stride that fits into your travel schedule.

When you are riding mile after mile, hour after hour in a bus, car, train, or riverboat, you can be lulled into thinking that not much is happening. Keep your book in your lap and make small sketches showing the character of the countryside you pass. Every now and then, or when things change, begin a new sketch. You will catch people and barns and haystacks in vignettes. On a city tour a vignette page is an opportunity to collect a few hints of what you saw from the bus.

Going from Phoenix to the Grand Canyon by car, I made eight full double pages of changing landscape in addition to the sights we stopped to see. I did en route sketching on the long trip from La Paz, Bolivia, to Cusco, Peru, and on to Machu Picchu. I made three horizontal strips to a page, like ribbons, page after page, in order to show the extraordinary scenery and life along the way. They read like comic strips and tell a great story.

GROUP TRAVEL

An organized tour is ideal for Sketchbooking. You are free from having to drive, read maps, pay bills, etc. Because your schedule is determined by someone else, your time is freed up for sketching. Although you may not have as much time as you would like, you *do* have time to sketch!

Other people on a tour don't care what you do as long as you're not keeping them waiting. Your sketching soon will become rou-

PERU

4/23/87
4:00PM

127

17 — TOWN OF JULY WHERE WE ENTERED PERU — ON THE SHORE OF TITICACA

18

TOPIARY IN THE PLAZA — BIG SEA GULL
we stopped here to change money
INTIS 22 = $1.

23 — Slept at the Tourist Hotel in Juliaca, as planned.

NEXT MORNING...
ON THE PLAZA AT
JULIACA — BEFORE WE
CAUGHT THE TRAIN TO
CUZCO.

1

April 24

← WE ASK WHAT WAS IN HER PACK + SHE UNLOADED !

tine to them. Early in the trip, find an appropriate time to assure the group that, although you will often sketch until the last minute, you will NEVER hold them up. Telling them defuses anxiety, both theirs and yours. Also mention that they might be in your book. People are usually delighted to be in a sketch, no matter how abstractly.

When people are sitting around chatting, you can unobtrusively take out your book and sketch. While they are shopping, draw the shop. When you are waiting for the group to assemble, or when the guide is giving lengthy, interesting explanations, sketch! Use whatever time you have.

Staying caught up is a challenge because so much happens on a tour. If you get behind with too many unfinished sketches, settle down somewhere and catch up. If you are constantly falling behind, perhaps your drawings are too complex. Try to keep your sketches simple—draw the doorway instead of the whole cathedral.

If you miss a day or two of sketching, leave a blank page so you can write a bit about the missed events. Resume sketching and continue your story. Experience shows that leaving pages blank to fill with sketches later rarely works.

Your sketching and your book are going to generate interest from others in the group, attention you might not want. When someone asks to look at your book, you can explain that you would like for them to see it, but later, when it is farther along. My advice is to not let even your mother see it until you are well in to the book! People will ask if they can watch you sketch. You can say, "I hope you will understand, but having someone watch me sketch

Sketch people while they are involved in an activity. These whale-watchers don't know (or mind) that they are being sketched.

opposite: This "enroute sketch" records a long day of traveling in Peru.

51

makes me nervous." (A polite way to say "Go away!") People will enjoy talking to you about your work, and you can have pleasant encounters both with other travelers and with people of the places you visit. Your book is an avenue of communication, and you can open or close it as you wish.

In foreign lands, people will be especially curious about your work. In Tanzania, a Masai took my pen and added an ornament to his hair on my sketch. The average tourist has little opportunity, other than buying something, to talk to the locals. You can have a wonderful time "talking," whether or not there is a language barrier. This aspect of Sketchbooking is one of the best rewards of travel sketching. The vendors pester others in the tour group; strangely, they do not try to sell me anything. I asked one Peruvian street vendor, who was looking over my shoulder, what was in her pack. She happily emptied it on the sidewalk before me. She was delighted when I made a tiny sketch of it.

SAVING PAPER

If you worry about running out of paper, you will soon stop sketching. Use paper freely. While using pages of vignettes and strip sketches may, in fact, save paper, the real reason to use them is that they are appropriate to the situation. I have found, miraculously, that a trip fits into a book without a conscious strategy to make it happen.

Sketching provides occasion for communication if you wish. People on this boat told me I should go forward and meet the other artist on board— a four-year-old boy. We were both delighted with the encounter.

VICTORIA DEL LAGO
The catamaran we
traveled on in the
Nahuel Huapi Lake

Holding crackers for the gulls.

ON THE
BOAT

Frederico,
Cuatro años
de B.A.
A fellow artist! He is drawing me,
while I draw him.

Try to have your book as finished as you can by the time you get home. Before other things start to crowd your schedule, make a quiet time to READ your book. Make any corrections, additions, improvements, and add color where it suits you. Put a photo of yourself and your companions on the page opposite the title page. Put the title on the spine of the book. Add it to your growing library of sketchbooks.

This travel sketchbook is a personal expression of your encounter with places, people, and experiences. It is a unique document, a treasure—a work of art! Put the book on the coffee table for others to enjoy.

CAMPSITE BAY OF FUNDY STATE PARK

sketched while Bob read my Journey Journal aloud

CHAPTER FIVE

And Finally…

By this time, you are proving to yourself that you can make all kinds of sketches. You have the ability and the desire. Yet everything and everyone on earth seems to be conspiring to keep you from doing it! All the demands of the day, all the distractions of modern society, will take priority over what you want to do for yourself. Your art is last on the list, and if you are not careful, it will fall right off!

The value of creating sketchbooks is more than you realize when you are first starting out. You learn and grow in the process of Sketchbooking; you never know what good ideas it will generate in yourself or in others. You are creatively engaged in the production of an art form. Sketchbooking helps develop the ability and sensitivity to respond to moments that enrich your life.

You do not drift into being an artist, any more than you drift into a trip around the world, or a college education. You set up for it. Then you dive in.

Ready, set, go SKETCHBOOKING!

AGRIDOME
SHOW

They all smile all the time
Very sweet

19 different kinds

Shorn on:
1 Merino
2 Perendale
3 Dorset Horn

Sheep shearing demo
"Relax" natur"

"For food I'll stand
up in front of all those
laughing people"
thinks The
sheep

MERINO

CORRIEDALE

Border Leicester

southdown

Sheep on display

45

The Mc...

Try to have at least one sketch of everything you do on your trip. This drawing documents the many different varieties of sheep seen at an agridome show in New Zealand. Although it seemed impossible to draw, I wanted to include the event in my story.

Include your adventurous activities in your sketchbook. This sketch shows us getting soaked by a giant wave while river rafting.

US↑

HANG ON FOR YOUR LIFE! THREE TIMES WE WERE SOAKED BUT THIS WAS THE WORST--- JUST LIKE THE GREAT WAVE OF KANAZAWA by HOKUSAI.

It's fun to note the unusual things you see. This is how some fathers babysit in Nepal.

Papa baby sitting   Nepal

Low tide in the Upper Salmon River at Alma, New Brunswick. Sometimes a simple line sketch, without shading or color, is all that's needed to capture a scene.

in the distance
our campsite overlooking
Upper Salmon River
at Alma, N.B. 4-7-81   Tide's out!

59

Keep sketching, even in seemingly impossible situations. This day at Stonehenge was terribly windy and cold but I drew us there anyway.

DRIZZLE + SUN BRIGHT SUN
May 17 and GUSTS TO 75mph!
LOST MY SCARF
BLOWN AWAY
AT STONEHENGE wow!

plastic ponchos
85

Getting into rowboats to see sunrise on the Ganges River. Extraordinary experiences are brought to life through the on-the-spot sketches you manage to get.

Getting into row boats to see sunrise on the Ganges

STANDING AT THE MIDDLE OF THE EARTH····
A FOOT IN THE NORTHERN HEMISPHERE, AND A FOOT IN THE SOUTHERN

Sketchbookers Reporting In!

Remarks adapted from students' comments:

- I remembered you saying, "Don't quit on a bad sketch; keep on anyhow." The resulting sketch was the one people like the best. A tour company used it in their next brochure.
- The sketch you least expect will tell you the most later…the tail of the cat disappearing as he goes behind the wood stove brings back the ambiance of a visit with dear friends in Ireland.
- Two sisters write that the sketchbook of their first vacation together as adults is an extraordinary document. It brought them closer together, recording the great fun they had in Key West.
- The only way I can get a rest on the long, long hikes we take is to stop for a sketch. This my husband will accept, but the idea of stopping for a rest is out of the question. He enjoys seeing the sketches develop.
- Sketching every day does wonders for my creativity.
- I learned to use the whole three minutes.

- I always wanted to draw. I'm doing it!
- Sketchbooking has been a revelation to me. It has shown me many possibilities, given me permission, helped me to counteract my overly fussy instincts, and more! In addition to making travel more fun, I think it will help me become a better painter.
- Every sketch I've added to that blue-bound sketchbook, whether the awkward incomplete ones or the finished not-so-bad ones, has more power than the best photograph to bring back the experience that prompted it.
- Your "go ahead, do it, enjoy it and don't worry about perfection" approach was exactly what I needed. Sketching has added a new and enjoyable dimension to seeing and a clearer realization that "quick" is not necessarily synonymous with "careless."
- One thing about sketching, everyone wants to see what you have done. If you want to understand the people of different cultures, it is a nice way to make a connection. Children are especially interested in your drawings of them. It's a good way to cross cultural barriers.
- I take exotic vacations, hiking on Machu Picchu or climbing Mount Kenya. I carry a sketchbook to capture, among the clicking cameras, the exhilarating moments in my own unique way. And, a sketchbook is lighter than a camera! It costs less, too.
- It's expanding my capacity for art.
- I learned not to be intimidated by anything.

- My husband photographed, I sketched. It will be interesting to see, ten years from now, how the pictures we each "took" look to us in hindsight. At least my narrative will serve as a story line for his pictures.
- Until you showed me that sketching is for my pleasure, not for inspection by others, I was afraid to draw. You have opened up a whole new world for me.
- I recorded the mundane and special moments—only to find after the summer ended that they were all special moments.
- I keep my sketchbook handy in the most frequented spot in my life: the car. It takes the edge off the anxiety of waiting because I get utterly absorbed; but more importantly, I'm learning all about surroundings I thought were familiar to me.
- The lessons of Sketchbooking were that I really do have time enough, and space enough, and skill enough, with relatively simple materials, to produce something that will be meaningful to me. And this work can be part of my life with other people, even an addition to it, not a distraction from it.

BARBARA STECHER developed the concept of Sketchbooking to better observe things that interest her. She enjoys the storytelling aspect of "being there" that shines through the pages. She loves the outdoors and has introduced hundreds of people to the pleasures and value of observing through sketching.

She teaches two courses—*Sketchbooking* and *Watercolor for Travelers*—at the DeCordova Museum School of Art in Lincoln, Massachusetts. Occasionally, she takes groups on Sketchbooking trips abroad. She has traveled, sketchbook in hand, to more than 70 locales from the Antarctic to Nepal. She has a degree in education from San Diego State University, a degree in painting from Old Dominion University, and a Masters in Art History from American University. She currently works as a research assistant at DeCordova.

Barbara Stecher